HAL LEONARD

PIANO METHOD

JAZZ PIANO FOR KIDS

A Beginner's Guide with Step-by-Step Instruction for Jazz Piano

BY RICHARD MICHAEL

PLAYBACK+
Speed • Pitch • Balance • Loop

To access video visit:
www.halleonard.com/mylibrary

Enter Code
2934-3296-0469-1571

ISBN 978-1-5400-6780-7

Visit Hal Leonard Online at
www.halleonard.com

Contact us:
Hal Leonard
7777 West Bluemound Road
Milwaukee, WI 53213
Email: info@halleonard.com

In Europe, contact:
Hal Leonard Europe Limited
42 Wigmore Street
Marylebone, London, W1U 2RN
Email: info@halleonardeurope.com

In Australia, contact:
Hal Leonard Australia Pty. Ltd.
4 Lentara Court
Cheltenham, Victoria, 3192 Australia
Email: info@halleonard.com.au

DEDICATION

This work is dedicated to Robin, Joanna, and Hilary. Having been dragged along to their Dad's workshops as children, they could well have written this book themselves!

RM - 2021

INTRODUCTION

Welcome to *Jazz Piano for Kids* and your very first steps in making up your own solos. What do you need? Apart from a piano or keyboard, just two hands, two wide-open ears, and the ability to have a go without fear of making mistakes. This beginner's course will give you the building blocks of playing jazz on the piano. Your only critic is yourself, and that's where the ears come in. Carefully work your way through the accompanying videos. Before you know it, you will be improvising your own solos and starting a lifetime's discovery in the wonderful world of jazz.

A WORD FOR THE KIDS

This book and its videos are designed to get you improvising and feeling the freedom that comes from knowing your way around a chord sequence. This is not a book about just playing the piano. However, the author strongly advises all players to check in with a teacher to learn about posture, fingering, pedalling, and all the other skills required to play the piano. These basic elements of piano technique are important whatever the style of music you feel passionate about. They are all explored in the book *Piano for Kids*, published by Hal Leonard.

A WORD FOR TEACHERS

My sincere hope is that you can use the techniques outlined in this book to encourage your pupils to develop skills in improvisation. Even if you know next to nothing about jazz, the various chapters will explain its building blocks to you and your pupil. As a teacher, you can address the aspects of piano playing that are not covered within these pages, but you can also develop improvising skills yourself. What's not to like?

Chord symbols are included in all the blues and standard tunes as a resource for teachers who wish to accompany the pupil on piano or guitar. This book is not a harmony textbook, but explanations of how chords are formed are included in the latter pages. J.S. Bach insisted that all his pupils improvise, and emphasised the skill in his teaching. Now, if it's good enough for Bach. . .

HOW TO USE THIS BOOK

This is no ordinary piano book! At the heart of an authentic jazz education is listening and playing, copying and creating. The focus in most piano methods is on *notation*, which is learning to read and perform music accurately from a written score. Here, the focus is on *improvisation* (although notation is also covered). This is the art of making up music as you play. How do you do that then? This book is packed with videos specifically designed to get you listening, copying, and improvising. Make your way through the book at a pace that suits you, playing back the videos as many times as you wish. Before you know it, you'll be well and truly in the groove! Listening and playing, copying and creating. It's the way every great jazz musician learned.

To access the accompanying videos, simply go to www.halleonard.com/mylibrary and enter the code found on page 1 of this book. This will grant you instant access to every file. You can download to your computer, tablet, or phone, or stream the videos live. This feature is available exclusively from Hal Leonard and is included with the price of this book!

For technical support, please email support@halleonard.com

ABOUT THE AUTHOR

One of the UK's leading jazz educators and an authority on improvisation, pianist and composer Richard Michael can look back on a distinguished career that began as a child playing in his father's Scottish country dance band. These early stages proved to be the building blocks in a career that has seen Richard awarded the British Empire Medal for services to music education in the Queen's Birthday Honours in 2012. He was Jazz Educator of the Year in 2011 in the Parliamentary Jazz Awards, and many of his students have gone on to become leading jazz musicians.

Leaving full-time class teaching in 2007 to follow a freelance career, Richard became a leading figure in the development of the ABRSM's Jazz Syllabus and is currently a regular broadcaster on BBC radio, dissecting and analysing the music of the jazz masters. He gives recitals on the history of jazz piano, and is equally at home improvising fugues on the organ.

Richard's albums are available from his website richardmichaelsjazzschool.com, and he has many published compositions. He has been working with violinist Nicola Benedetti on the Benedetti Foundation, is Honorary Professor of Jazz Piano at St Andrews University, and organist at Abbotshall Church, Kirkcaldy, where he lives with his wife Morag.

CONTENTS

GROOVE

Before you play a note, let's think about the magic ingredient in all music. It's called groove.

Without groove, music just doesn't happen. Groove can be taught, felt, and developed in everyone. Every time you listen to music with four beats in the bar, feel where the beats are and clap in time. If you are in the groove, you will clap on "2" and "4." If you are not in the groove, you will clap on "1" and "3." Which are you?

Let's find out in our first video.

 Ex. 1: Clapping the Groove

We're now going to play a great clapping game to get us in the groove. Look at this next video and follow the instructions. You can download the notation too if this is useful.

 Ex. 2: Clap    Ex. 2 Notation

How did you get on? We're going add a beat now and step this game up a notch! Look at this next video and follow the instructions. Again, if it's useful to see the notation, you can download that here.

 Ex. 3: Clap-Slap    Ex. 3 Notation

We're not done! Watch the next video, where we add in another beat. The notation can be downloaded here.

 Ex. 4: Clap-Slap-Stamp    Ex. 4 Notation

How do you feel? You should be counting all the time and feeling that groove. In the next video, let's crank up the tempo and run all three rhythm games without a break. Play it through as many times as you like until you are really in the groove!

 Ex. 5: Rhythm Games

Before moving to the piano, let's do some *echo clapping*. I will clap, slap, and stamp a one-bar phrase, which you will copy. I'll then move on to a two-bar phrase and ask you again to copy my actions. This is echo clapping.

 Ex. 6: Echo Clapping

Now, let's do *call and response*. When I create a one-bar phrase, instead of copying it as with an echo response, make up your own. Then do the same thing with a two-bar phrase. Remember, less is more, so you don't have to fill up every space!

 Ex. 7: Call and Response

Let's try out your groove on the piano using the techniques you just learned.

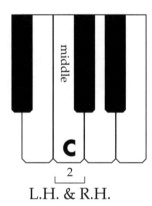

left hand
(L.H.)

L.H. & R.H.

right hand
(R.H.)

Using the second fingers of each hand playing middle C, we will do *echo playing* on a one-bar phrase, then a two-bar phrase. Echo playing is copying in the same way as we did earlier with echo clapping, except now using notes!

 Ex. 8: Echo Playing

You have been improvising using just one note, how cool is that? Now I'm going to accompany you in your first solo. Follow my directions on the video, get in the groove, and play!

 Ex. 9: First Solo

SINGING A GROOVE

When you play a solo on the piano, you must project by making it sing in the way great vocalists (like Frank Sinatra or Ella Fitzgerald) projected their voices to us via live or recorded performance.

Let's practise this idea by singing two grooves and improvising with our voices and bodies. It's not as daft as it sounds! The two grooves we are going to sing and take solos on are *swing* and *rock*.

Listen to any jazz track that has a swing feel and the drummer will almost certainly be playing a particular rhythm on the hi-hat. See if you can imitate it with your mouth using the syllables "Cha **Chi-Chi** Cha **Chi-Chi**." Copy me on this next video.

1 **2**   3 **4**

 Ex. 10: Swing Groove

That's the sound of a swing groove, with the main accents coming on beats 2 and 4.

We are now going to learn *four-way independence* (meaning hands and feet can do different things at the same time) and become drummers using our bodies as the drumkit. Sit comfortably with both feet on the floor and put your hands on your legs.

Watch me and copy. Take your time to master each part. Do not be surprised if you have to repeat this example quite a few times before it feels secure. If you'd like to use notation too, this can be downloaded here.

 Ex. 11: Swing Groove: Hands and Feet   ⬇ Download   Ex. 11 Notation

STRAIGHT AND SWING

You might notice that the quavers/eighth notes on all our notation are written *straight*. This means they look like they are the same length. Unless indicated, we are going to clap and play them *swung*. This means the first in each pair is actually longer than the second.

1 & 2 & 3 & 4 &
long - short   long - short   long - short   long - short

Let's turn to a rock groove. In the swing groove we've just played, each quarter note/crotchet beat is divided by three to give that swing feel. It's instantly recognisable. If you walk on the spot and repeat the name "Cam-er-on" to each beat, you will hear that the beat is divided into three. Do the same thing with the name "Ro-bin" and you will hear that the beat is divided into two. This how we divide the beat in a rock groove.

With our voices, we will sound like a bass drum by saying the word "Goong." The snare drum will be a short "Ka" and the hi-hat "Chi." Although this looks like a foreign language, it works, and is the language of rock.

Copy me and away we go onto the next video, saying "Goong Ka Chi Goong Ka Chi."

                                     1   2   3 4

 Ex. 12: Rock Groove

Let's now play a rock groove with hands and feet. As in the swing groove, you may have to repeat this many times before it feels secure. If it is helpful, notation can be downloaded here also.

 Ex. 13: Rock Groove: Hands and Feet  **Ex. 13 Notation**

It's time for solos. But first, let's work on the *count-in*, the means by which jazz musicians indicate the speed and feel of the piece they are going to play. This is hugely important, so just watch the next two video examples and copy my voice exactly, using the inflexions I give when counting in.

 Ex. 14: The Count-In (1)

 Ex. 15: The Count-In (2)

In the next example, we will play a swing groove for three bars and then improvise a *fill* in the fourth bar using hands, feet, and voice. A fill is a short improvisation a drummer uses at the end of a phrase. Notation for both exercises can be downloaded.

 Ex. 16: The Fill: Swing Groove  **Ex. 16 Notation**

 Ex. 17: The Fill: Rock Groove  **Ex. 17 Notation**

HOW WE HEAR THE CHORDS CHANGE

If you played a recording of any great song to a stranger, it's certain the first thing they would notice is the tune or *melody*. However, as jazz musicians, we're as interested in the bit underneath, which is called *harmony*.

Harmony is more than one note sounding at the same time. A *chord* usually consists of a group of notes played together. Playing jazz piano is really nothing more than playing a tune, with chords and a bass line! However, to really understand and master this skill, let's investigate further. Watch the video and follow the music along as you do so.

 Ex. 18: The Rhythm Song

THE RHYTHM SONG

Here's the tune all on its own, with lyrics.

Rhy - thm, we got rhy - thm. Rhy - thm, we got rhy - thm.

Rhy - thm, we got rhy - thm. We got rhy - thm all day long.

Rhy - thm, we got rhy - thm. Rhy - thm, we got rhy - thm.

Now, let's add a bass part.

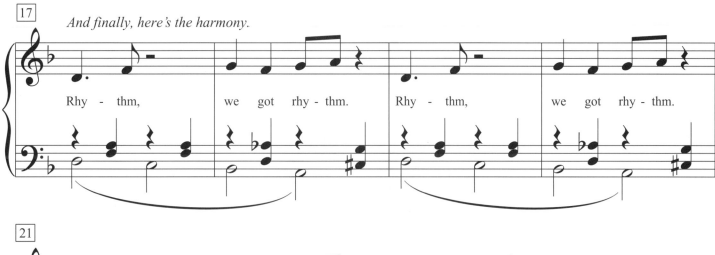

And finally, here's the harmony.

Could you hear the three separate parts of this song?

To help you, I'm now going to play a variety of different tunes and I want you to *hear* when the harmony changes.

 Ex. 19: Hearing Harmony

It's your turn. You're going to play the harmony to a *12-bar blues.* The 12-bar blues is the most common chord sequence there is in popular music, and you can play this with your right hand or both hands.

With your right hand, play middle C-E-G with fingers 1-3-5.

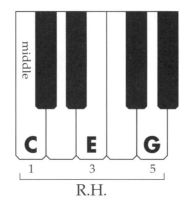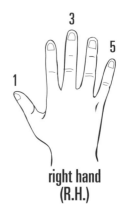

Or, play middle C with finger 2 of your left hand and, with right-hand fingers 2 and 4, play E and G.

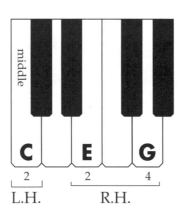

Try both ways and decide which is most comfortable for you. C-E-G played together is a C major chord.

When you are ready, move your hand (or hands) four keys higher, so that you are now playing F-A-C. This is an F major chord.

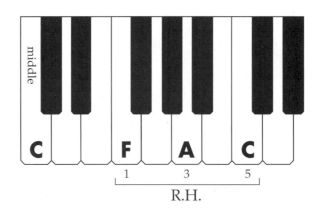

Move one key to the right again to G-B-D and you have a G major chord.

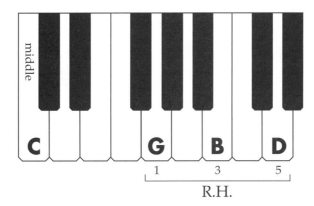

With these three chords in your repertoire, you can play a 12-bar blues in the key of C major. Watch the video as I demonstrate this for you.

 Ex. 20: 12-Bar Blues

Once you can move comfortably round the three chords, you are ready to start playing your first 12-bar blues and a *standard* (the word *standard* is given to especially popular and well-known tunes).

STRENGTHENING THE FINGERS

You will never see a professional golfer hit a drive before warming up. Similarly, any athlete will always ensure that arms and legs are all warmed up before any action takes place. It's the same with playing the piano.

Here's my favourite exercise to get your fingers moving. Start with right-hand thumb on Middle C, and left-hand finger 5 on the C one-octave lower. In the next video, I demonstrate this in the right hand only, but you can do it in both hands simultaneously.

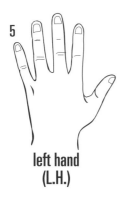

left hand
(L.H.)

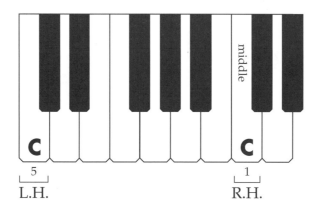

L.H.   R.H.

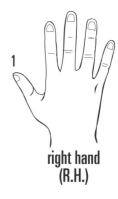

right hand
(R.H.)

 Ex. 21: Warm-Up 1

It's your turn! Follow the instructions in the next video and you'll be nicely warmed up to start improvising.

 Ex. 22: Warm-Up 2

PLAYING TUNES AND SOLOS

From now on, you are going to learn to play and take solos on 10 blues and 10 standard *chord sequences* (a chord sequence means a progression of chords, one after another). First, you need to know the language jazz musicians use when playing.

A TYPICAL STANDARD STRUCTURE

The structure of each of the blues and standards we are going to play is based on this simple idea.

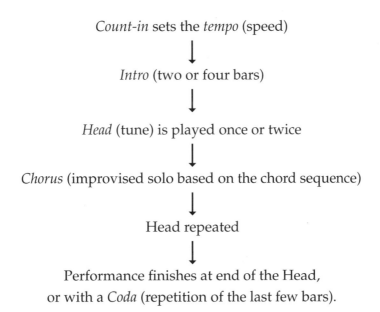

Count-in sets the *tempo* (speed)

↓

Intro (two or four bars)

↓

Head (tune) is played once or twice

↓

Chorus (improvised solo based on the chord sequence)

↓

Head repeated

↓

Performance finishes at end of the Head,
or with a *Coda* (repetition of the last few bars).

Sometimes, you might come across the direction, *D.C. al fine*. This just means, "go back to the beginning and finish where it says *fine*."

You are going to play every piece in this book using the videos, learning alongside me. For all 20 examples we are going to play together, the structure will be the same. I play the piano over a backing of keyboard, bass, and drums. Here's the structure:

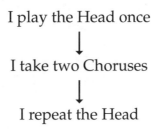

I play the Head once

↓

I take two Choruses

↓

I repeat the Head

Then, when you're ready, you do it yourself, following exactly the same structure as I accompany you!

FINGER NUMBERS

A word about fingering! You'll notice in the notation that I have made fingering suggestions, all designed around a basic hand position. Your hand can stay in the same position for most of the song. Some places in the music notation show where the left hand can also be involved to make movement around the notes easier. When a finger number appears above the note, play it with your right hand. When a finger number appears below the note, play it with your left hand. When appropriate, you'll also see a keyboard with fingering marked on it. This will help you to visualise the principal fingering for the piece you are about to play. The fingering I've suggested has been designed specifically to make each piece as accessible as possible. However, the finger numbers are still only a guide. Reasonable alternatives are possible. Indeed, I experiment with some in my videos, as you'll no doubt notice.

left hand
(L.H.)

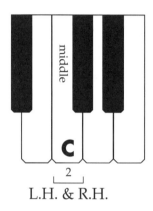

L.H. & R.H.

right hand
(R.H.)

SKILL IMPROVISING SKILLS

With each blues and standard tune you will learn, there will be a new technique to develop your skill in improvising a solo. Look out for the sign **SKILL** and you'll know you are about to learn a new skill.

Improvisation is not about playing any old note. It's like an interesting conversation in which subjects are developed and shaped. Always keep this in mind as we learn together. Come on, let's try it!

SOLO TIME 1: ANTICIPATION

BLUES 1

For this first tune, we'll keep it nice and simple. "Blues 1" uses only one note until the ninth bar. It's where the notes are played that enables you to create the music. You can play the note C with either the second finger of your right hand or alternate between the second fingers of both hands. Once you listen to my performance, you will soon understand how to play the piece. When you feel ready, go on to replace my solo part with your own.

**left hand
(L.H.)**

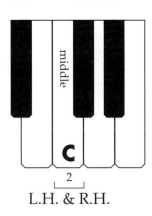

middle

C

2

L.H. & R.H.

**right hand
(R.H.)**

SKILL

This tune introduces us to *anticipation*. This just means starting a phrase slightly before any of the four beats in the bar.

After this, the backing for each tune is repeated and *you* take my place as leader and soloist. Off we go!

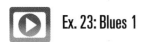

BLUES 1

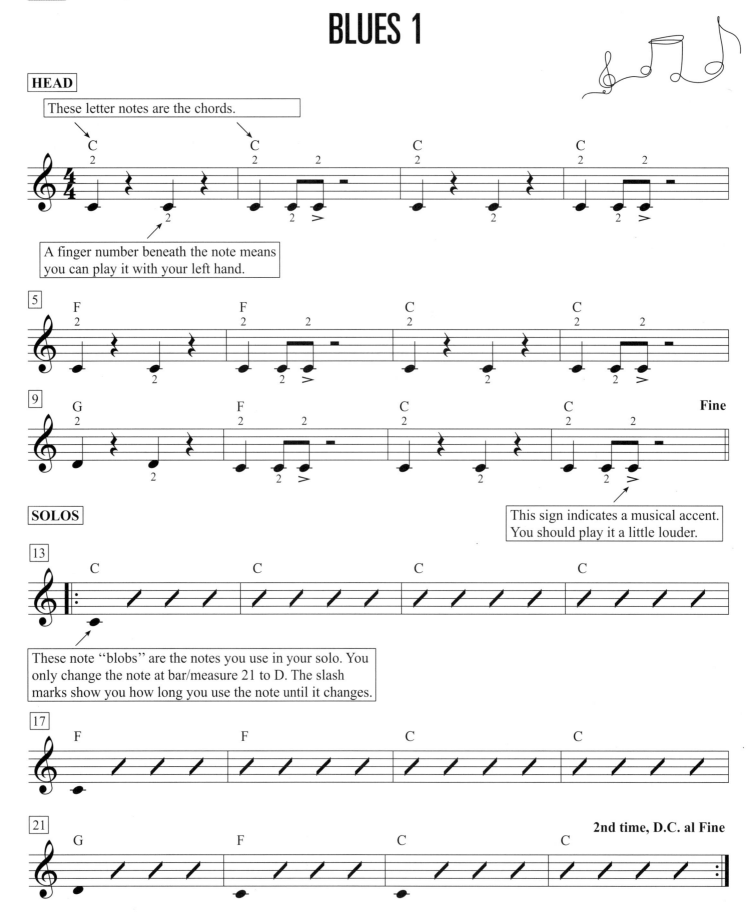

HEAD

These letter notes are the chords.

A finger number beneath the note means you can play it with your left hand.

This sign indicates a musical accent. You should play it a little louder.

SOLOS

These note "blobs" are the notes you use in your solo. You only change the note at bar/measure 21 to D. The slash marks show you how long you use the note until it changes.

On the video, you will hear me play the tune once then take two choruses. After a pause, it's your turn playing along with the band.

GO TELL AUNT RHODY

This is an American folk song harmonised with two chords, C and G. Can you hear when they change? When you play your solo, try to hear the chords in your head. Remember that some of the greatest jazz, folk, and classical musicians learned their craft by ear, and some (like pianist Erroll Garner) never learned to read music at all!

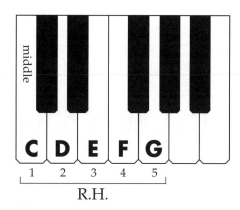

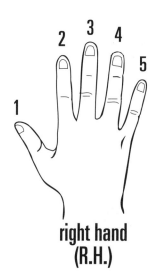

right hand
(R.H.)

Ex. 24: Go Tell Aunt Rhody

GO TELL AUNT RHODY

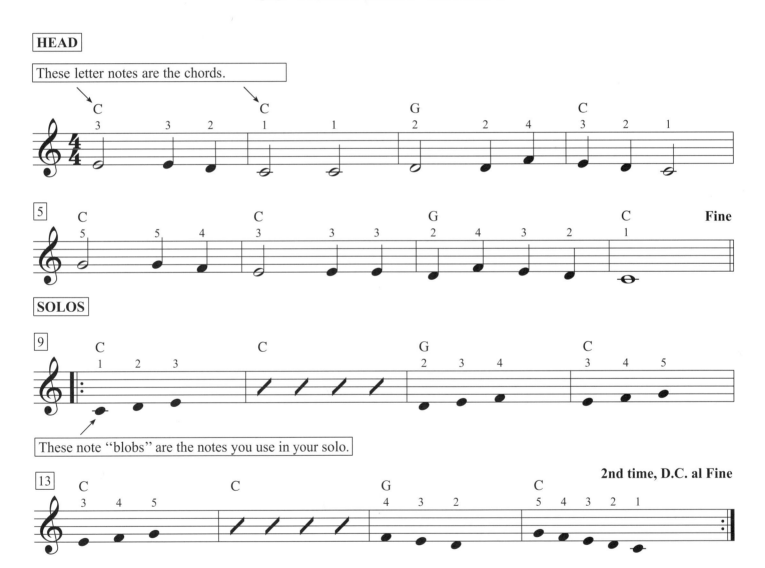

On the video, you will hear me play the tune once, then improvise twice on the chords
before playing the tune again. After a pause, it's your turn playing along with the band.

SOLO TIME 2: INVERSION

BLUES 2

This uses the same rhythm as "Blues 1," but this time the tune is spread over three notes, which are the first three notes of a scale we will use as a tool for improvising our solo.

SKILL

The skill we will use here is called *inversion*. This means to repeat a musical idea, but change all the intervals going up to intervals going down (or vice versa). We'll examine this in the next video. You can, if you wish, use your left hand in this piece. For fingering, instead of using "1" of your right hand, you could use "2" of your left hand.

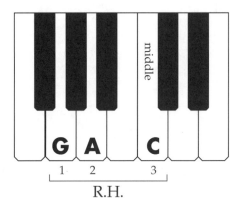

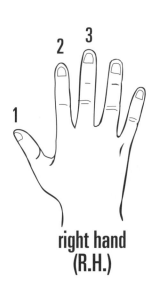

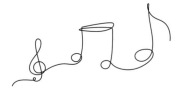

BLUES 2

LA CUCARACHA

This is in a rock groove and is a traditional Spanish folk song about a cockroach who cannot walk!

"La Cucaracha" is harmonised with C and G, like "Go Tell Aunt Rhody." But here, the chords change at different times. It is so important that you can hear when these changes occur, as anticipating the chord changes as you play is one of the big differences between classical and jazz piano. In classical piano, a high standard can be reached without hearing when the chords change. In jazz, it is impossible to reach any standard without learning this skill.

The first three notes of "La Cucaracha" begin before the first bar. As you hear me count in, you'll notice the count is "1-2 , 1-2-3" and then you have the first three notes of the tune! This is known as an *anacrusis*, but jazz musicians call it a *pick-up*. Listen to my recording and try it yourself.

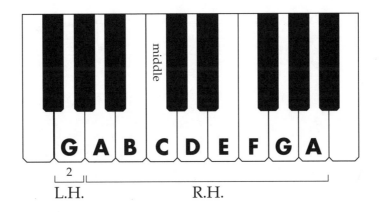

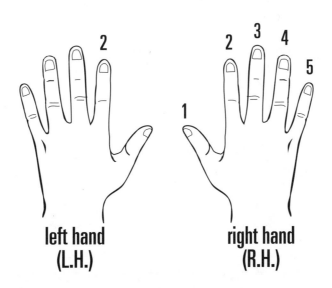

LA CUCARACHA

A finger number beneath the note means you can play it with your left hand.

SOLO TIME 3: REPETITION

BLUES 3

This uses the same rhythm as "Blues 1" and "Blues 2" but explores a different area of the scale to improvise on a 12-bar blues.

SKILL

The technique we will use here is called *repetition*, meaning when you play an idea, play it again! After three times, you then move on to another idea. You can again use your left hand in this piece. Instead of using the thumb of your right hand, use the second finger of your left hand.

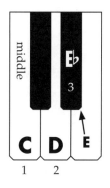

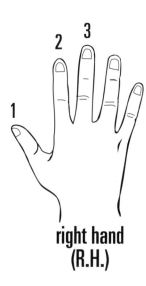

**right hand
(R.H.)**

Ex. 27: Blues 3

BLUES 3

Here we have a repetition of *the first 2 bars.*

26

THE RHYTHM SONG

This is an original tune, using a repeated bass figure called an *ostinato*. An ostinato is a persistently repeating musical pattern.

 Ex. 28: The Rhythm Song

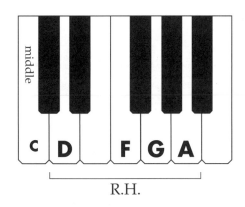

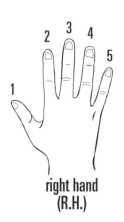

THE RHYTHM SONG

SOLO TIME 4: SCALE TONES AND TRANSPOSITION

BLUES 4

For this tune, the notes we have learned are now joined up to make a scale known as an *altered pentatonic*.

Oh yeah, big deal! Somehow that seems complicated, but it's just a term used to describe a scale that musicians have used since jazz began. And here's how it has evolved. If you can play five different sports, you are a pentathlete. A pentagon has five sides. So, you can see that the word "penta" refers to anything to do with the number five.

Similarly, a five-note scale is called a *pentatonic scale*. The black keys on the keyboard make up a pentatonic scale. If you start on any black key, for example F♯, and play only black keys until you reach F♯ again, you've played a pentatonic scale!

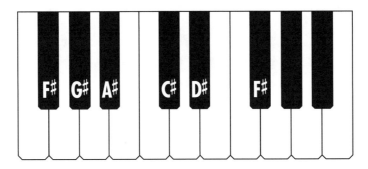

To play a pentatonic scale on white keys, start on middle C and move in an ascending order: C-D-E-G-A. That is a pentatonic scale on C.

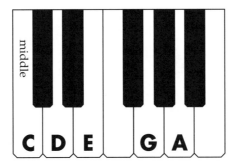

Now play D-E-G-A-C, then E-G-A-C-D, then G-A-C-D-E, then stop!

Each of these patterns are versions of a C pentatonic scale. It's the last one that has a jazz sound if we make one small change.

In a pentatonic scale, there are no half steps (semitones). If you raise or lower any of these notes, the scale is then known as an *altered pentatonic*. If we flatten the top E to E♭, we now have the scale that is used in "Blues 4." Wow! Basing improvisations on just the notes of a scale is known as using *scale tones*.

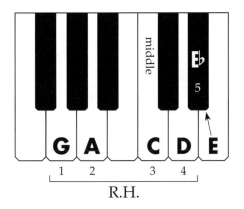

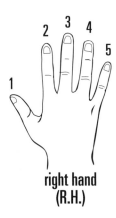

SKILL

Now we can practise the technique of *transposition*. In music, to transpose means to take a block of music (chords, melody, or both) and repeat it in a different key. In the next video, we are going to break the altered pentatonic into two parts (or *areas*) and improvise in both areas using the technique of transposition in "Blues 4."

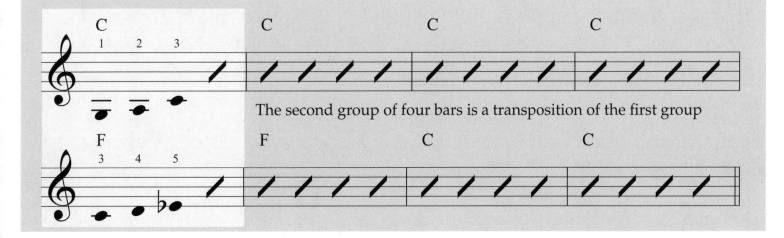

The second group of four bars is a transposition of the first group

BLUES 4

MICHAEL ROW THE BOARD ASHORE

This is an American Spiritual dating back to the mid-19th century. In this simplified version, we have just three chords: C, F, and G. However, when you are more experienced, add in the E minor chord (in brackets) associated with this song. As you play, try to hear when the chords change. In no time, you will start to hear this instinctively. In the last four bars of the solo, keep the same hand position but move (that is, transpose) it to the next set of pitches as the chord changes for each bar.

TRANSPOSITION IN MICHAEL ROW THE BOAT ASHORE

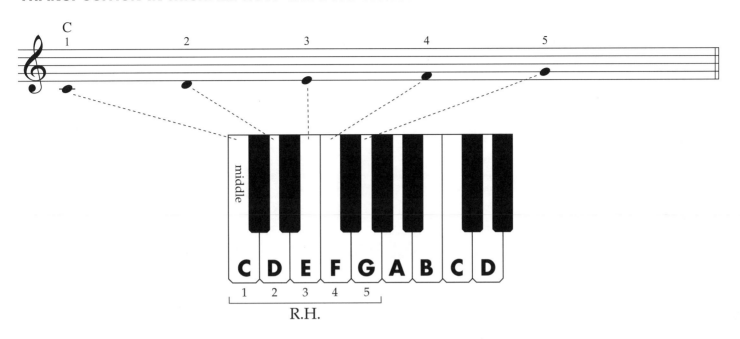

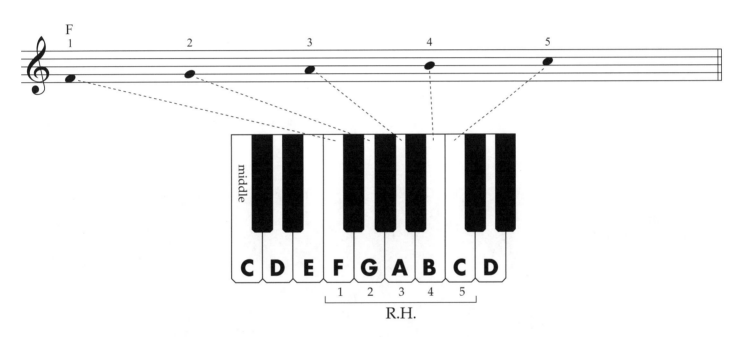

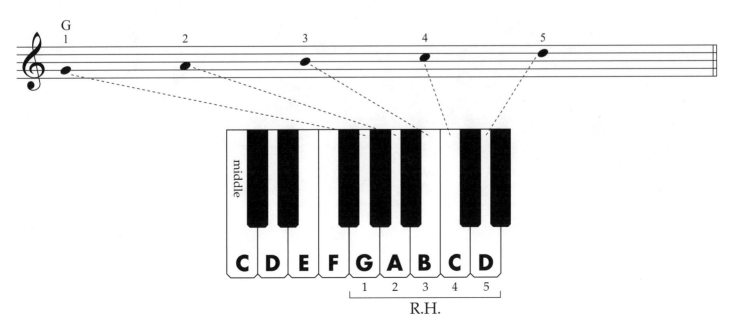

MICHAEL ROW THE BOAT ASHORE

SOLO TIME 5: CHORD TONES AND THE SEQUENCE

BLUES 5

Let's move from improvising using scale tones to using *chord tones* (the notes that make up a chord). In "Blues 5," keep the same hand position when the chord changes from bar 1 to bar 5 and then throughout the tune.

On the second chorus, combine what you have learned from "Blues 1-4" on scale tones with the chord tones in "Blues 5."

SKILL

The technique we will use here is called *sequence*. A sequence is a melodic device, where a pattern of notes is repeated at a higher or lower pitch. Think of the second part of the well-known Christmas carol "Ding Dong Merrily on High," where the melody on the word "Gloria" repeats itself, getting lower every time. This is a sequence.

Sequence (same melodic pattern, repeated at a lower pitch)

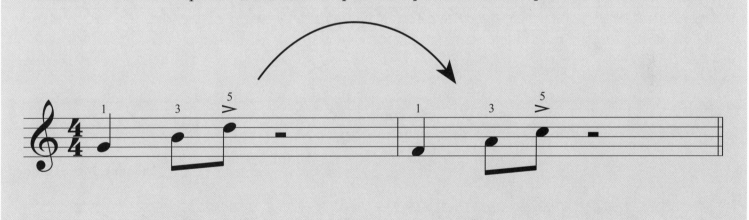

BLUES 5

These two bars make up a sequence. Bar 10 on this music is the same as bar 9, just a step lower.

JINGLE BELLS

This just has to be the one tune that everybody knows! Now it's time to hear it as a jazz musician and see how the chord sequence is constructed. We are still using just C, F, and G chords, but it's *where* they change and what they change *to* that is important. For the purposes of this book, we are only using the chorus and not the verse.

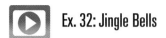 Ex. 32: Jingle Bells

JINGLE BELLS

SOLO TIME 6: GUIDE TONES AND HAND SHIFTING

Now for a complete change in your playing, as the left hand is added to play a new technique called *guide tones*, accompanying your right-hand solo.

So, what is a guide tone? Quite simply, it's the note in a chord that creates a feeling of tension (*dissonance*), leaning toward another guide tone, creating a release of tension (*consonance*).

In the following video, I'll show you an easy way to hear this lovely effect. We'll also combine this with creating a *vamp*. The word *vamp* is used by jazz musicians to describe a constantly repeated rhythmic figure supported by chords. In classical music, it is often called an *ostinato* and in pop music, a *loop*! Make up your own rhythms to create a vamp. Hopefully, the next video example will inspire you to experiment!

 Ex. 33: Guide Tones

BLUES 6

This introduces another scale used in jazz called a *minor pentatonic*. In this kind of pentatonic scale, our five notes are spread out like this: C-E♭-F-G-B♭-(C).

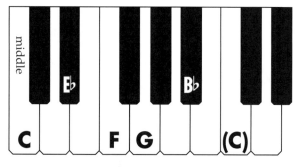

The hand position you have used before won't work here as the notes are more spread out. So let's learn about *hand shifting*. With your right hand, play C, E♭, and F with fingers 1-2-3, then shift your thumb under your third finger to play G, B♭, and high C with fingers 1-2-3.

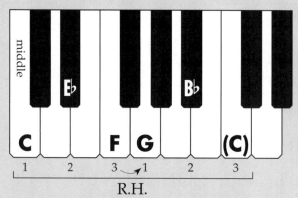

That's the fingering for the minor pentatonic scale going up. Coming down, cross finger 3 over your thumb. Practise playing the C minor pentatonic scale with this fingering slowly, and then move to "Blues 6."

Ex. 34: Blues 6

BLUES 6

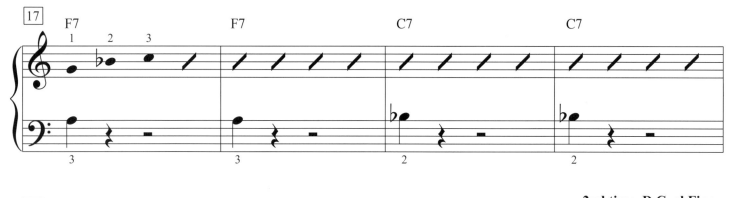

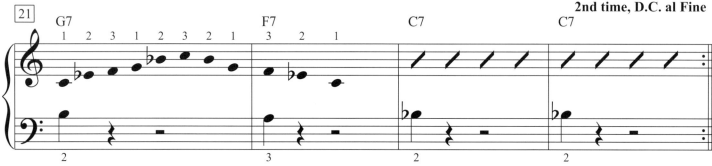

> Notes with a dot (.) under the note head should be nice and short, detached from the next note. Notes with a dash (_) under the note head should have weight and a bit more length.

NOBODY KNOWS THE TROUBLE I'VE SEEN

This is another American Spiritual. Among the many recordings of this lovely song, is one by the great jazz innovator, trumpet player, and singer Louis Armstrong. If you can listen to this version, you will learn so much about how to feel jazz.

You might notice that the harmony in "Blues 6" moves away from the basic chords of our first five standards. For now, your left hand will just keep playing guide tones. We'll learn more about these jazz harmonies in the following chapters.

In the opening bars of the right hand, you will see a curved line over the notes. This is a *phrase mark* and signifies a musical sentence. When you finish speaking a sentence, you take a breath. It's much the same in music. Notice that when I get to the end of a phrase mark, I take a "musical breath" by taking my hand off the piano!

In the left hand, there are groups of two notes with a curved line over them. This is called a *slur*. This is different from a phrase mark because it indicates smooth articulation. At the end of the slur, you make a small break. You can see an example of these markings below.

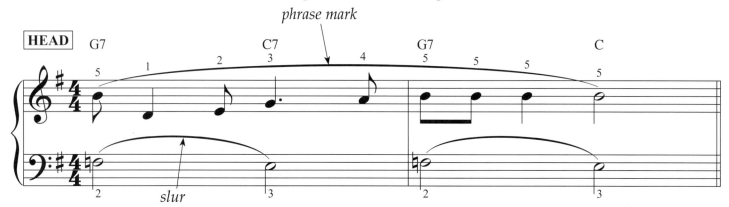

Ex. 35: Nobody Knows the Trouble I've Seen

NOBODY KNOWS THE TROUBLE I'VE SEEN

SOLO TIME 7: AUGMENTATION AND THE BLUES SCALE

BLUES 7

So far, your scale vocabulary includes the pentatonic, altered pentatonic, and minor pentatonic. Let's add one more note to the minor pentatonic to create what is known as the *blues scale*. Here it is with the new note in bold.

C-E♭-F-**F♯**-G-B♭-C (high)

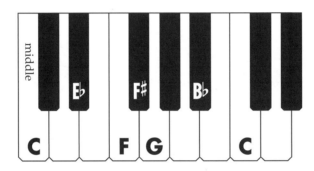

Why is it called the blues scale? With your left hand, play C below middle C and hold down E and B♭ above the C to form a C7 chord. Play the notes of the blues scale over this chord.

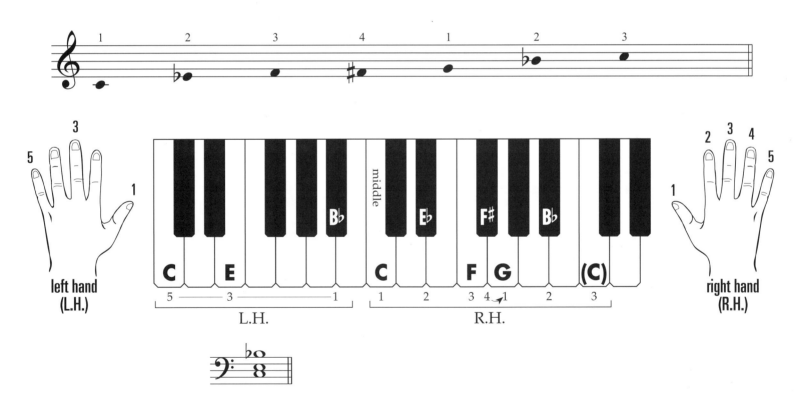

Wow, this scale is really cool! It is cool because of the E♭, F♯, and B♭. They are not part of the natural C major scale, and are called *blue note*s. It is from these notes that the blues scale gets its name.

The left hand in "Blues 7" plays the same rhythmic figure throughout, but feel free to make up your own rhythm when you play the solo. Practise playing the right-hand opening phrase slowly, passing your thumb under your fourth finger.

Here's one more thing to consider before we hit the next tune, and that is the technique of *augmentation*. This is taking a musical idea and repeating it, but using longer rhythms. Listen to my example on the video and you'll get it.

Ex. 36: Blues 7

BLUES 7

2nd time, D.C. al Fine

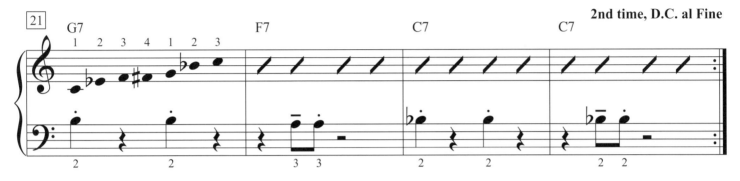

SHE'LL BE COMIN' 'ROUND THE MOUNTAIN

This is a traditional American folk song, which in Scotland is known as, "Ye Canna Shove yer Granny aff a Bus!" This tune starts with a pick-up, and I'll count you in on the video.

 Ex. 37: She'll Be Comin' 'Round the Mountain

SHE'LL BE COMIN' 'ROUND THE MOUNTAIN

SOLOS

2nd time, D.C. al Fine

44

SOLO TIME 8: DIMINUTION

SKILL

In the last chapter, you learned the technique of augmentation. Now, you will learn the opposite, *diminution*. Diminution means to repeat a phrase using the same note pitches, but shorter note values. You are also going to use a *turnaround*, which is a harmonic device that "turns round" the chord changes at the end of a solo to enable the next chorus to start more effectively.

You'll catch onto both these ideas easily by watching the next video.

CODA

You will see from "Blues 8" onwards that we will use a coda. When you repeat the head after the solos, simply follow the directions in the music to the $\oplus$ CODA at the very end of the piece.

CHORD TONES IN BLUES 8

In "Blues 8," the pitches given in your solo section indicate the four notes of each chord in the blues: *root* (first note of the chord), third, fifth, and flat seventh. The three chords these pitches outline are:

C7

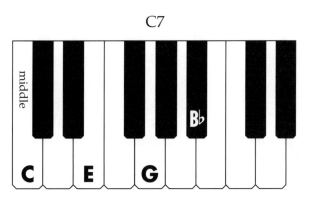

F7

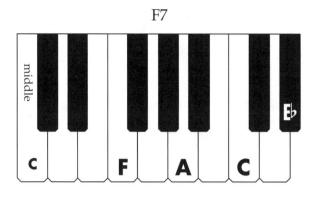

G7

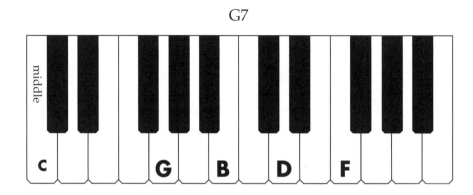

Remember, as you work on "Blues 8" you can also use all the other techniques and scales you've learned as you wish.

Ex. 38: Blues 8

BLUES 8

SOLOS

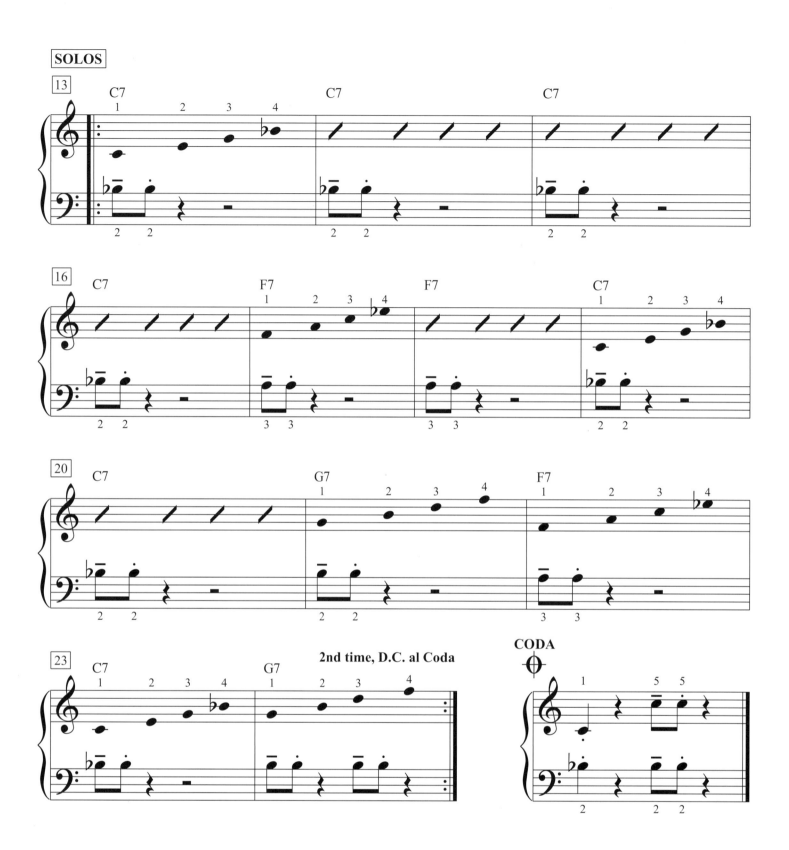

2nd time, D.C. al Coda

CODA

MARCH

One of the greatest writers of tunes was the Russian composer Pyotr Il'yich Tchaikovsky, although he probably never imagined that one of the tunes from his ballet *The Nutcracker* would feature in a book about jazz piano!

What's interesting about "March" is that the first half of the tune stays in the home key of G Major. Then, the fun begins as Tchaikovsky moves away to the keys of E Minor (bar 12) and D Major (bar 16).

This is known as a *modulation* (which means to change key). Just like life would be unexciting if you only ever stayed in your hometown, without the musical journey of modulation, music would be dull and boring. That key signature at the start of a tune only tells you what key you start in. Before long, most melodies have a *middle eight* where the tune changes key. Jazz musicians build up a repertoire of middle eights over many years and can recognise by ear where a tune is going, and when it has landed in a new key.

At the end of "March," there is a coda where I play what is known as a *Basie ending*. The great pianist and band leader Count Basie loved to finish tunes with his signature ending of three short chords.

 Ex. 39: March

MARCH

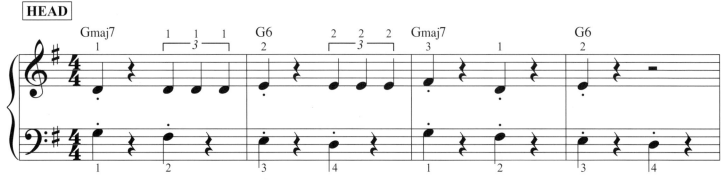

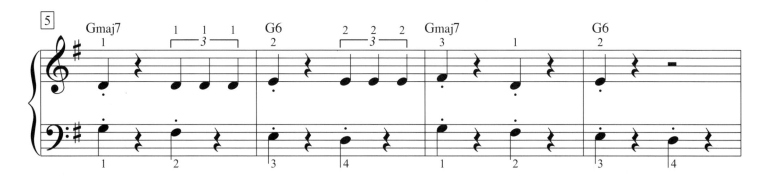

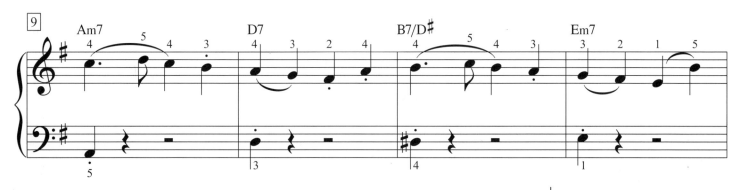

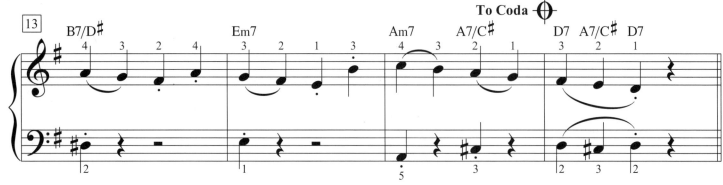

SOLO TIME 9: JAZZ HARMONY AND SPACE

It's time for us to learn just how uncomplicated harmony is! First, you must become familiar with the different jazz-chord qualities you find in a major scale.

In the key of C, let's give the chords numbers from 1 to 7. (For some reason, roman numerals are often used to label chords. We'll stick to plain old numbers for now.)

Chord 1 is C-E-G-B and is C major seventh (Cmaj7)

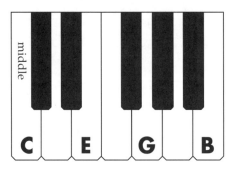

Chord 2 is D-F-A-C and is D minor seventh (Dm7)

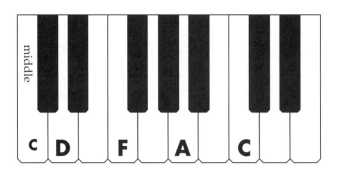

Chord 3 is E-G-B-D and is E minor seventh (Em7)

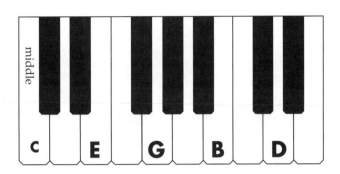

Chord 4 is F-A-C-E and is F major seventh (Fmaj7)

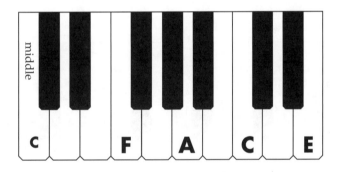

Chord 5 is G-B-D-F and is G seventh (G7)

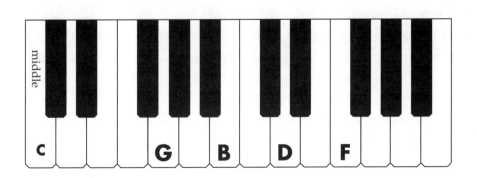

Chord 6 is A-C-E-G and is A minor seventh (Am7)

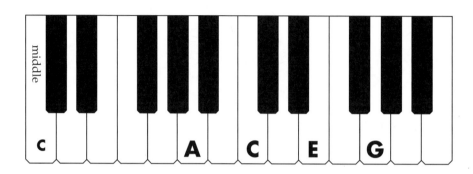

Chord 7 is B-D-F-A and is B minor seventh flat five (Bm7♭5)

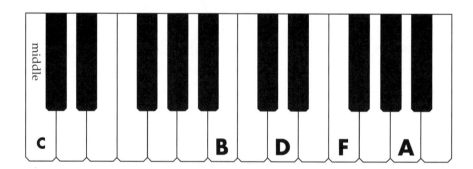

You can see that Chords 1 and 4 are *major sevenths*. Chords 2, 3, and 6 are *minor sevenths*. Chord 5 is just *G7* (or a *dominant seventh*), and Chord 7 is a *minor seventh with a flat five* (this just means the 5th of the chord is lowered by half a step). This is the same in any major key.

So, really there are only four *qualities* of chord! All the music we call jazz is constructed around these four chord qualities. These are the important ones that you need to know about at this stage in your journey through jazz piano. The chord names can sound intimidating, but in time you will be able to identify them by ear and by sight. Listening and playing makes understanding harmony second nature!

THE FOUR CHORD QUALITIES

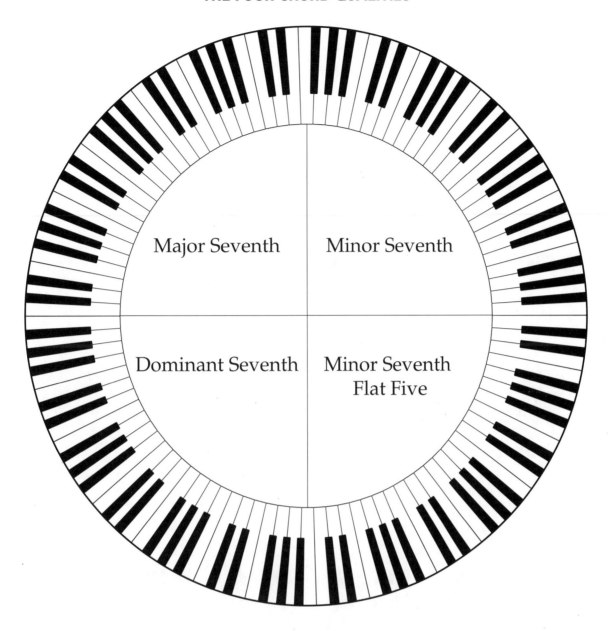

It's time to listen and play this harmony in the next video.

 Ex. 40: Jazz Harmony

BLUES 9

There's just one last scale to learn in the blues! This is called the *mixolydian* scale. To play this scale, just play the *scale notes* over the chords C7, F7, and G7. (*Scale notes* are the notes that make up the scale related to the chord.) You'll learn how to do this in "Blues 9" by watching the next video. The scale notes are also marked on the keyboards below, with fingering.

MIXOLYDIAN SCALE ON C

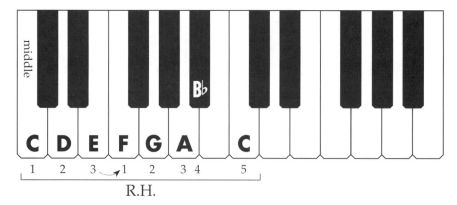

MIXOLYDIAN SCALE ON F

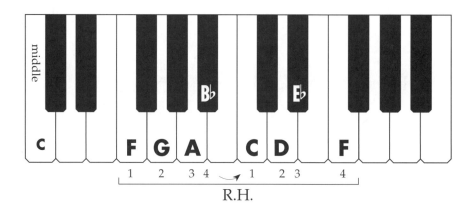

MIXOLYDIAN SCALE ON G

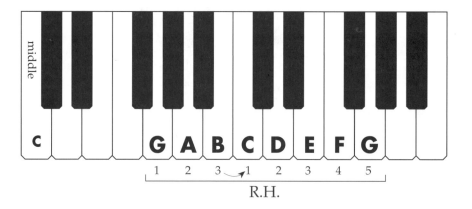

SKILL

The improvisation technique we will use when playing "Blues 9" is simply called *space*. "You don't get paid by the note," is an old musician's saying. Never be afraid to allow space into your improvisation. Let your ideas breathe.

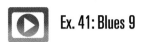 Ex. 41: Blues 9

BLUES 9

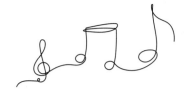

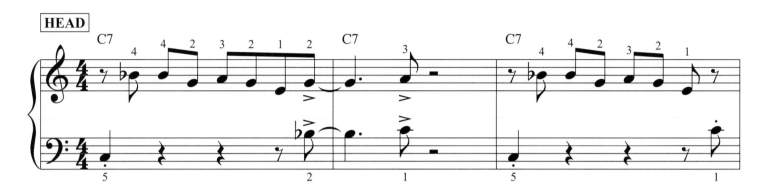

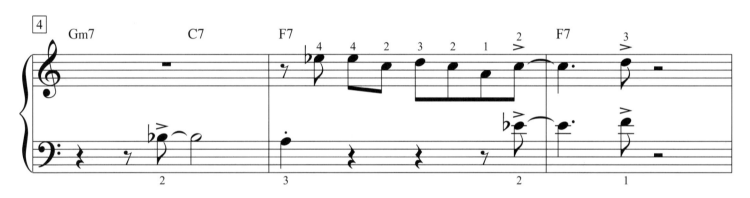

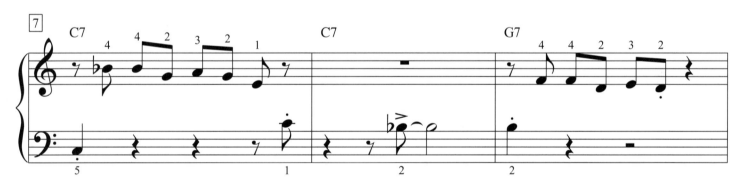

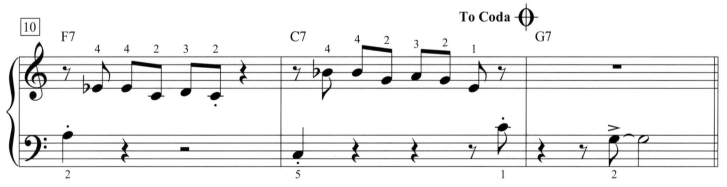

SOLOS

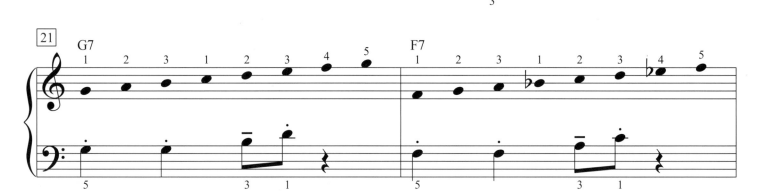

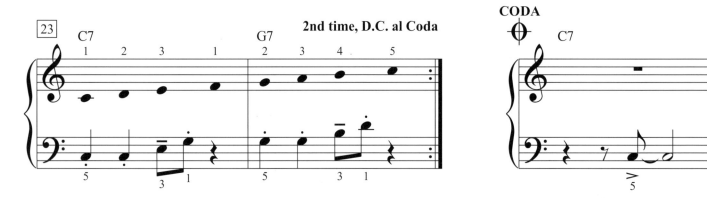

2nd time, D.C. al Coda

CODA

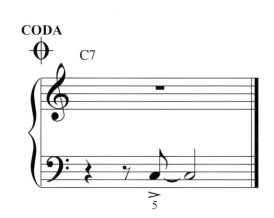

PAGANINI'S GROOVE

Niccolò Paganini (1782-1840) was the most brilliant violinist of his day and wrote many pieces for the violin. One of the best known is his "Caprice No. 24," which many composers have used as a basis for a *theme and variations*. In a way, most jazz performances up to the late 1950s were just theme and variations. It is essentially another way of describing what we know as head and choruses!

The tune is given a swing treatment here, and the middle section is a perfect example of the 2-5-1 chord progression. In fact, this section alone contains the same chords you will find in the opening bars of the well-known jazz standard "Autumn Leaves."

PAGANINI'S GROOVE

SOLOS

SOLO TIME 10: PUTTING IT ALL TOGETHER

BLUES 10

In this piece, the mixolydian scale we've learned about is used throughout the head. For our final blues piece, there are no pitches indicated. Use all the techniques you have learned when you take your solo (although not all at once)! Don't be afraid to make mistakes, "there are none." And that's a quote from the great jazz trumpeter, Miles Davis.

You have more notes to play in "Blues 10." Here's why we all have to practise scales. As your knowledge of improvisation grows, so must your technique! The secret of developing a good piano technique is to practise slowly and in time.

The left-hand accompaniment uses two guide tones which are the third and seventh of the chords. Although they are written as whole notes, play them in any rhythm you feel is natural to you.

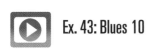 Ex. 43: Blues 10

BLUES 10

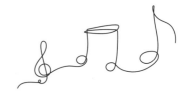

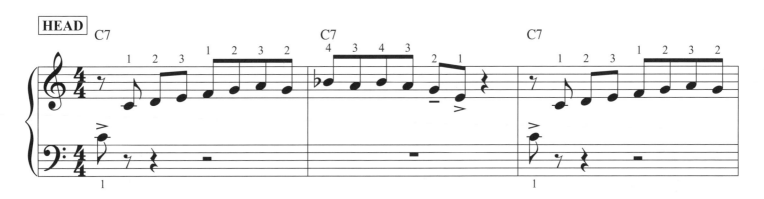

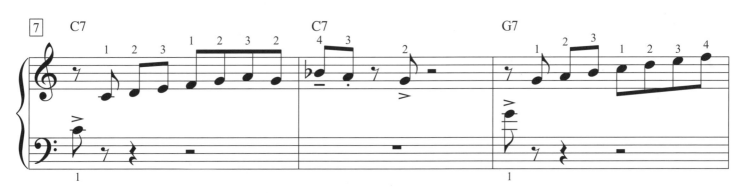

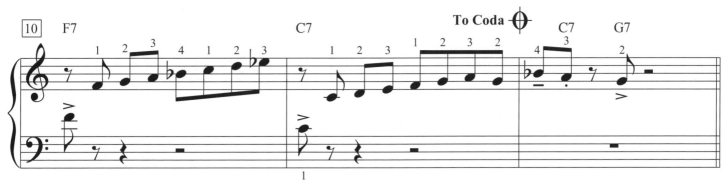

63

2nd time, D.C. al Coda

CODA

WHEN THE SAINTS GO MARCHING IN

We finish our trip through the standards by playing a tune recognised the world over. There are many versions of this song, but for the definitive performance, turn again to that of the great Louis Armstrong.

This is the first standard in the book that has an *intro*. An intro is just a means of setting up the piece using material that will appear later in the arrangement. You should now have the confidence to play through this arrangement using all the techniques learned in the preceding chapters.

WHEN THE SAINTS GO MARCHING IN

WHAT NEXT?

We have gone on quite a journey together. But for you, this is just the beginning! The late trumpet player and educator Clark Terry said that learning jazz was a matter of, "imitation, assimilation, and innovation." In other words, improvising is just like learning to speak. You copy the sounds you hear from your parents before you learn to read. You then absorb these sounds and, before long, you are able to speak and communicate. With music, the process is exactly the same. You must listen as much as you can to recordings by the great jazz musicians of the past and present. As a jazz-mad teenager, my pocket money went on LP records and as many jazz publications as were available at the time. Had YouTube, Spotify, iTunes, or any other media streaming services been available to me as I began my journey through improvisation, it's doubtful whether I would have learned to read and write with the availability of music on tap!

Never be afraid of getting it wrong. My hope is that this wee book has given you the building blocks and the desire to create your own music, embracing a lifetime of creativity and enjoyment. Many congratulations on taking the important first steps in your journey with jazz. Here's a little something extra to show you just where this could lead.

 Bonus Video

Certificate of Achievement

Congratulations to

_____

(YOUR NAME)

_____

(DATE)

You have completed

JAZZ PIANO FOR KIDS

_____

(TEACHER SIGNATURE)

HAL•LEONARD®

HAL LEONARD METHODS FOR KIDS

This popular series of method books for youngsters provides accessible courses that teach children to play their instrument of choice faster than ever before. The clean, simple page layouts ensure kids' attention remains on each new concept. Every new song presented builds on concepts they have learned in previous songs, so kids stay motivated and progress with confidence. These methods can be used in combination with a teacher or parent. The price of each book includes access to audio play-along and demonstration tracks online for download or streaming.

GUITAR FOR KIDS, METHOD BOOK 1

by Bob Morris and Jeff Schroedl

This method is equally suitable for students using electric or acoustic guitars. It features popular songs, including: Hokey Pokey • Hound Dog • I'm a Believer • Surfin' USA • This Land Is Your Land • Yellow Submarine • and more.

00865003 Book/Online Audio.............................$12.99

GUITAR FOR KIDS, METHOD BOOK 2

by Chad Johnson

Equally suitable for children using electric or acoustic guitars, this book picks up where Book 1 left off. Songs include: Dust in the Wind • Eight Days a Week • Fields of Gold • Let It Go • Oye Como Va • Rock Around the Clock • and more.

00128427 Book/Online Audio.............................$12.99

GUITAR FOR KIDS: BLUES METHOD BOOK

by Dave Rubin

Cool blues riffs, chords and solos are featured in this method, which is suitable for children using electric or acoustic guitars. Lessons include: selecting your guitar • parts of the guitar • holding the guitar • hand position • easy tablature • strumming & picking • blues riffs & chords • basic blues soloing • and more.

00248636 Book/Online Audio.............................$12.99

GUITAR FOR KIDS SONGBOOK

This supplement follows chords in the order they are taught in book 1 of the guitar method. 10 songs: At the Hop • Don't Worry, Be Happy • Electric Avenue • Every Breath You Take • Feelin' Alright • Fly like an Eagle • Jambalaya (On the Bayou) • Love Me Do • Paperback Writer • Three Little Birds.

00697402 Book/Online Audio.............................$9.99

GUITAR FOR KIDS METHOD & SONGBOOK

00697403 Book/Online Audio.............................$19.99

Prices, contents, and availability
subject to change without notice.

BASS FOR KIDS METHOD BOOK

by Chad Johnson

Topics in this method book include selecting a bass, holding the bass, hand position, reading music notation and counting, and more. It also features popular songs including: Crazy Train • Every Breath You Take • A Hard Day's Night • Wild Thing • and more. Includes tab.

00696449 Book/Online Audio.............................$12.99

DRUMS FOR KIDS METHOD BOOK

Topics included in this method book for young beginning drummers include setting up the drumset, music reading, learning rhthms, coordination, and more. Includes the songs: Another One Bites the Dust • Crazy Train • Free Fallin' • Living After Midnight • Old Time Rock & Roll • Stir It Up • When the Levee Breaks • and more.

00113420 Book/Online Audio.............................$12.99

HARMONICA FOR KIDS METHOD BOOK

by Eric Plahna

Lessons include topics such as hand position, basic chord playing, learning melodies, and much more. Includes over 30 songs: All My Loving • Happy Birthday to You • Jingle Bells • Over the River and Through the Woods • Scarborough Fair • Take Me Out to the Ball Game • This Land Is Your Land • You Are My Sunshine • and more.

00131101 Book/Online Audio.............................$12.99

PIANO FOR KIDS METHOD BOOK

by Jennifer Linn

This fun, easy course incorporates popular songs including: Beauty and the Beast • Heart and Soul • Let It Go • Over the Rainbow • We Will Rock You • and more classical/folk tunes. Topics covered include parts of the piano, good posture and hand position, note reading, dynamics and more.

00156774 Book/Online Audio.............................$12.99

PIANO FOR KIDS SONGBOOK

by Jennifer Linn

A supplementary companion to the method book for piano, this book presents classic songs and contemporary hits which progress in like manner with the method book. Includes: All of Me • Can't Stop the Feeling • Do Re Mi • Linus and Lucy • and more.

00217215 Book/Online Audio.............................$12.99

PIANO FOR KIDS CHRISTMAS SONGBOOK

by Jennifer Linn

Includes: Go, Tell It on the Mountain • I Want a Hippopotamus for Christmas • Jingle Bell Rock • Jingle Bells • Mary, Did You Know? • Rudolph the Red-Nosed Reindeer • Up on the Housetop • We Three Kings of Orient Are • and more.

00238915 Book/Online Audio.............................$12.99

UKULELE FOR KIDS

by Chad Johnson

This book features popular songs including: Barbara Ann • The Hokey Pokey • Rock Around the Clock • This Land Is Your Land • Yellow Submarine • You Are My Sunshine • and more. Lessons include: selecting your uke; parts of the uke; holding the uke; hand position; reading music notation and counting; notes on the strings; strumming and picking; and more!

00696468 Book/Online Audio.............................$12.99

UKULELE FOR KIDS SONGBOOK

Strum your favorite hits from Jason Mraz, Disney, U2 and more! This collection can be used on its own, as a supplement to the *Ukulele for Kids* method book or any other beginning ukulele method. Songs: Don't Worry, Be Happy • I'm Yours • The Lion Sleeps Tonight • Riptide • The Siamese Cat Song • and more.

00153137 Book/Online Audio.............................$9.99

UKULELE FOR KIDS METHOD & SONGBOOK

00244845 Book/Online Audio.............................$19.99

HAL•LEONARD®
www.halleonard.com